AF292461

One
Sun
We

Own.
What do we?

Here?

The blue path. The Red. The Green.

A watch tower.

We don't eat fish.

Neither moose.

Horizontal rain.

Lullabies are scary.

                                                              Do
the
                                      notes
exist?

Are
                                                                    they
like

                                      stars ?

All ready

                                                        vanished?

White and

                                      purple

flowers : a
                                      melody!

An
almost
blind

                                      dog.

                              An almond.

Like a rainbow in a curved air. Terry said.

I
don't
I
do

yet. Oh. Ah. Green? White. Green?

Reindeer.

Hey. No light is not
lame.

Darkness is a beautiful name.

But no heat...
The cold doesnt't reach our hearts.

Toward the red barn

and the synthesizers

dreaming
an
impossible
old
folk

song.

A fire could / grow / too

I can give you the light if you give me some bread:

Let's
make
a
sun
sandwich.

Toasted.

A baby with a big head.
A puppy making birds noises.

A bottle opened with a pen.

A toaster as a friend.

Only one window can be open.

The lamp is not helping.

I follow the trail in the woods, the wooden one, the one I am not
allowed to, the one that I will never take.

I am here and there now. My body splits in two like a log but no
one notice.
Or three.

It is so quiet.

How is it possible to tell. I won't.

I have two legs and so have you.
The spider has six.

The birches many hands.

White is the birch and my two legs.

I chose indian ink.

The grey eyes are blue.
The blue eyes are green.
The green eyes are brown.
The brown eyes are green.
The black eyes are blue.

I know.
It's easy.
You just have to understand that it is the same, the same that not
knowing.
And all of sudden, it opens widely.

And it burns.

LÀ. ICI.

The sky is too transparent and clear to see
anything else.

The curtains turns the light into something yellow.
I feed the mosquitos with my skin and blood.

A reward ?

The coffee is weak and disappointing as a 5th grade girlfriend.

We've been to the Redwoods.

I can tell.

The plastic dinosaurs too. The special coin. The girl at the cafe.

We don't talk about gender studies there. And also we are
(a young white straight couple)

Almost playmobils.
like them.
Are we coward?
What would have happened if we were not?
How come History is such a muted lady?

I fold the memory and its
quirky syntax in my pocket

And,

in my garlic hand
: the responsability of ackowledging the Avenue of the Giants
that we crossed.

The car may go
 inside
 the big tree.

A secret camp lay in the night.
Maybe some bikers.

I like Danny Lyon's portraits.
Ask him to be my uncle friend.
Can we?

Who are we?

One year after, eveyrthing was made of concrete.

In the concrete park with our friends
I chose one
concrete
animal.

In the shadow,

Without naming it. Pronouncing barely.

Eating basil.

Drinking ginger ale.

They moved their hands in silence. In a group of trees.

We were a few. They are many.

The dog is eating a piece of bird.

Those trees stand in the field like a psychedelic doom band on stage.
Hair down.
Serious.

Salt
rosemary
beer

a lozange

a triangle

e mails.

Lavandula latifolia.

How
Far
?

How true?
Danger / death / movies / fantasy?

Working door closed
is
the
sesame.

A nut, a castle, a curtain, playing an E key.

Watching is not staring is not gazing.

REGARDE
et ferme les yeux.

The twenties are gone. For me.

Beware then: Nostalgia begins. Une danse.

THE The
DANCE Dance
OF Of
THE The
PAST Past
FUTURE.
Future.

I swallow a mountain.
I inhale the birds' breath.

I digest peaks.

I hold in my brain the whole Washington state and can I walk in
every street of Chicago when I sleep?

I am in Finland. The same melody.

Do you know the Pomegranates?

Toi aussi.

The very light white flower that is hidden in the field, the very one
that we will never reach, think of, or see,

what
we
gonna
do
with
her?

Seriously!

In Hyrysalmi, 2012.

The very un-lighten cigarette?

Which
one
will
be
the
last ?

The unseen shooting star?

The very unsung song?

Warsaw? 1993?

I buy a cone without ice cream. I am 9.
A sandy road.
A wooden shack.
East European micro frogs.
Communism prices.

Most of the time, green.

I take

from the cardboard box
in this street of
Hudson
the ugly pair of blue shorts that are free

and a   melody.

If
I wear them in the Marina, the old men like

watching me. Walking.

Like I was
                                        a moving color

from the 80's.

I thraw them away in Seattle but keep whistling the anthem.

I was 28.

Mineral water.

Cascade.

Mineral Water.

Cassy and Effy.

Knees like rocks and hair like water.

The most beautiful wrists you would ever seen.

I've never been into animals until late.

Peeling fruits can be tiring.

Cucumbers.
Good.

Breathe. Getting old. How far are the 40's. The same glasses.
Jack Kerouac. Paris is dirty but they love it. A red dress. A white
dress. Are dresses overrated ? Her nails are covered with paint.
This is not a european quilt! Do they really buy this? I could.

European furniture doesn't exist.
Clear?

So i never asked. I always
speak.

Who
ask?

Who say? Who
speak?

Who is conviced?

Who is true? What
is
wrong?

Russian rivers crying over the falls.

I watch and spell the map with my finger but I don't read it.

I believe.

A park and a sandwich.
No one is wearing a watch. Who is wearing a ring?

Red nose, sundays secrets.

The swans mean more than what they actually are.

Their twisted neck. Do they know?

I send a dancing crab on the internet.

I give my love but i still have the same equivalent part of it inside.
This makes me
happy.

A sphere like a diamond chanting.

An animated sphere
An eerie choir.

I draw a heart.

An man from the past walking into a geodisc dome

I add colors to the folliage.

He is stuck
            forever
in

the A3 paper

Little bearded man from 1973,
I
will
make
photocopies

out ot you.

Now.

Topaz rags, cloudland ballroom Marfa Lights over mirrors.

I give my heart but i don't feel empty.

It comes back to me.

It's a love freesby.

85.

indie rock?

Contemporary art?

Cookies.

Maybe Zelda.

A walk to a lake or a higher building.

A morning or an evening.

Hair are beautiful when they are long.

Like a road, a river or a ribbon.

A dragon.

A hitch hiker.

The greatness of thumbs and fjords.

The Loch Ness one day.

Let me drive.
I will show you.

But I
don't
know
how
to
drive. Nothing. Neither
a car.
Nor
bicycles.

Nor
chewing gum bubbles.

But colored sketches.

And love.

The dark figures speak by the paint brush.
I break them and make them mine.

Sandals are pretty but they hurt.

The Holy Sprit, an ice cream and a violin.

I call the black power

and the transparent paper.

Painting is never wrong.

A circle on a square.

A circle is trust worthy.

A lemon pie can be disappointing.

Kandinsky made
a mistake and then he realized
it
wasn't
one. It was
modern art and theory.

In Kajaani I ordered the
wrong pizza.

Round, pink, yellow and red.

We took a picture of it. But we didn't
consumed

it.

They
made
comments.

Everything
is
abstract
and
not.

Here, in the blue forest. Near the watch tower.

Now you
might begin
to
understand.
Right?

No car, no leader, some beers, a thrift store somewhere.

Mind power.

Landscapes from above.

What about the giant and the old one. Do they?

After a while, she went through.

But, no cats.

A horse?

Dreaming is a bridge.

Easy doesn't mean easy.

Beautiful doesn't mean beautiful.

Hungry means hungry.

Storm means storm.

We don't go far : we are

all ready

                    there.

Applying
for
places.
Asking
for remoted rooms.
Taking trains.
Listening to mixes.

The joy of cooking.
Getting a hair cut is often a failure for girls.

The day light never stop coming back.

Virginia was. So was Silvia. They still are.
I cherrish them and add them to my pie. Oh, you writers ladies!

Her skin is transparent.
She is flexible.
She is rich.
She is immortal.

I couldn't afford it.

The actors always want to be singers, the singers want to be artists,
the artists want to be rich.

Some make music.

Let's make a pie.

A reindeer is twisting its neck, in silence.
I could be the reindeer.

A bad tv show is better than a bad movie. A bad american movie
is better than a bad french movie. A bad pizza is better than a bad
sandwich. A bad beer is better than a bad red wine.

I hold my hands into the light.

Landing on a piece of land
you've never been before.

I see a cloud from my window, i can't touch it and i want to cry.

I, getting older and happier every night?

In the mountains, where

Wyoming or Alpes, Appalaches, you see

Townes Van Zandt singing

the glory of the morning

and
eggs

I like pepper but

I am affraid of

i think of

and then, not

an unknown crystal can be frighting.

We should move more

but the notes are moving and
so are the leaves and
the salt in the pan

let's do it!

Sweet vampire
Beautiful teenager
Smart publicist
Faithfull doctor
Rich
The coffee is cold.

Did
you see?

I can feel
                              it.
Can you feel
                              it?

I am
sure

It is
going
to
be

                         good.

Félicia Atkinson
Twenties are gone

ISBN 9782365820035
SP021

Second edition of 700 copies

Published and designed by Shelter Press
www.shelter-press.com

Thank you Patricia De Peuter